Edible Object Talks

That Teach About
Values

by
Susan L. Lingo

STANDARD
PUBLISHING

Cincinnati, Ohio

Dedication
For the ear tests words as the tongue tastes food. (Job 34:3)

Edible Object Talks That Teach About Values
© 2000 by Susan L. Lingo

Published by Standard Publishing, Cincinnati, Ohio
A division of Standex International Corporation

All rights reserved. No part of this book may be reproduced in any manner whatsoever without written permission from the publisher, except where noted in the text and in the case of brief quotations embodied in critical articles and reviews.

Credits
Produced by Susan L. Lingo, Bright Ideas Books™
Illustrated by Paula Becker
Cover design by Liz Howe

All Scripture quotations, unless otherwise indicated, are taken from the HOLY BIBLE, NEW INTERNATIONAL VERSION®. NIV®. Copyright © 1973, 1978, 1984 by International Bible Society. Used by permission of Zondervan Publishing House. All rights reserved.

07 06 05 04 03 02 01   5 4 3 2
ISBN 0-7847-1183-6
Printed in the United States of America

The Menu

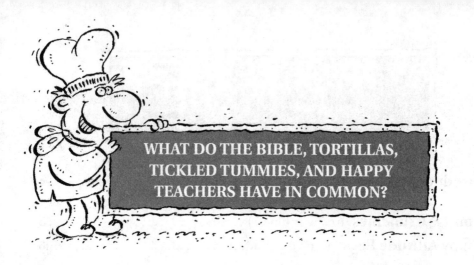

WHAT DO THE BIBLE, TORTILLAS, TICKLED TUMMIES, AND HAPPY TEACHERS HAVE IN COMMON?

Powerful Bible truths that are as nutritious to learn as they are fun to eat!

Edible Object Talks That Teach About Values is filled with twenty-five motivating, life-changing biblical messages served up in neat-to-eat treats that will help your kids devour and digest God's Word—and leave them shouting for seconds! In each memorable message, Chef Value introduces an important Christian value for kids to nurture in their lives, such as humility, love, acceptance, faith, and honesty. Kids interact with each message by reading from the Bible, discussing the importance of each value, and preparing simple snacks as tasty reminders of Bible truths. Kids come away from these message munchies filled with

- ❤ memorable reminders of God's Word,
- ❤ an awareness of Christian values in their lives,
- ❤ life-changing challenges for the upcoming week, and
- ❤ a sense of community and teamwork.

Use these neat-to-eat treats as motivating object talks, snack-time fun with a focus, or as super VBS together-times. Make every moment with your kids count as you present dynamic devotions they'll devour and memorable messages they'll digest!

(Please remember to check for possible food allergies before beginning *any* food activity.)

4

Promise Crunchies

THE VALUE DU JOUR:
Trustworthiness

OOD FOR THOUGHT

We can trust God's promises. *(1 Kings 8:56; Psalm 145:13)*

IMPLE INGREDIENTS

You'll need a Bible, marshmallow creme, crispy rice cereal, a large bowl, colorful candy sprinkles, plastic spoons, and 5-ounce plastic or paper cups (wax-lined). You'll also need access to a freezer. (If you would rather not freeze these treats, use the plastic spoons to simply eat them right from the cups.)

EVOURING THE MESSAGE

Hold up the box of crispy rice cereal and read aloud the label. Then ask kids what promises the cereal makers pledge, such as their cereal will be the crispiest, will taste better than others, is nutritious, or won't get soggy in milk.

Then prepare the Promise Crunchies as you discuss promises we often hear and how it feels when those promises aren't kept. Explain that you'll see if this cereal's promises are perfect. In a large bowl, have kids mix the following ingredients: a box of crispy rice cereal, a jar of marshmallow creme, and lots of candy sprinkles! Then take turns stirring the mixture until the cereal is coated and very sticky. Let kids spoon the colorful cereal mixture into their cups, then stick spoons in the center like lollipops. Place the treats in the freezer for half an hour (or let kids use the spoons to eat their treats now instead of freezing them).

Say: **We hear lots of promises every day—even down to the foods we eat! But these promises aren't always kept. In fact, there's only one person we can always trust to keep his promises and that's God! If God says cereal will be crunchy, we can trust that it will go crunch, crunch as we munch, munch! And when God says he'll love us forever, we can trust that we'll always be loved. Let's see what else the Bible tells us about God's perfect promises.** Read aloud 1 Kings 8:56 and Psalm 145:13. Then ask:

- How can trusting God's promises strengthen us? help our faith grow?
- Why does God keep his promises?
- What are some of God's promises to us?
- In what ways can we try to keep our promises just as God keeps his?

When the treats are frozen, tear away the cups and munch the goodies. Briefly discuss if the cereal stayed crunchy as promised. Then say: **God's perfect promises help us trust God even more. And trust leads to greater faith in God and his Word! We can also learn from God's loving promises and try harder to keep our word to God and to others. That's an important thing to do! Let's share a prayer thanking God for his perfect promises.** Pray: **Dear God, thank you for always keeping your Word so we can trust you more. Help us honor our promises, too. Amen.**

Encourage children to make these sweet treats at home for their families and friends to remind them that we can always trust God's Word—and that we need to be trustworthy, too!

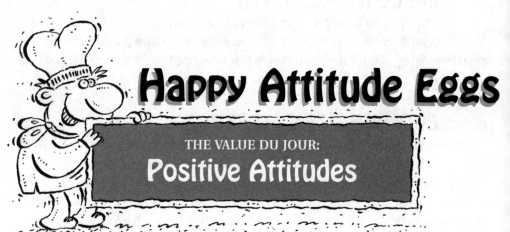

Happy Attitude Eggs

THE VALUE DU JOUR:
Positive Attitudes

OOD FOR THOUGHT

Attitudes are important to actions. *(Proverbs 15:30; Matthew 23:26)*

IMPLE INGREDIENTS

You'll need a Bible, newspapers, small bowls of slightly diluted food coloring, paintbrushes or cotton swabs, paper towels, a salt shaker, and one hard-boiled egg for each child plus one extra.

Before class, cover a table with newspapers and set out bowls of food coloring and paintbrushes or cotton swabs. Use plenty of food coloring in each bowl with only a bit of water—you want potent color for this snack idea!

EVOURING THE MESSAGE

Gather children and explain that you're going to make a tasty treat that will help them learn about attitudes and how they affect our actions. Hand each child a paper towel and a hard-boiled egg. Demonstrate how to carefully crack the eggs by tapping them on a table and then gently rolling them to make tiny cracks in the shells. Invite children to use the food coloring and paintbrushes or cotton swabs to "paint" their eggs—cracks and all! When the shells have been painted, wipe off any excess food coloring, then set the eggs aside for a moment.

Hold up the extra hard-boiled egg and ask kids to describe what they see. Say: **We all know this is an egg, but what do we really know about it? It's white, and it has a shell—but the shell keeps us from seeing what the egg is like on the inside. Does the inside match the outside? What if the outside shell was white, but the inside was black—would it be a good egg to eat? Probably not! We want an egg to be good both on the inside and the outside, just as we want to be as good inside as we are on the outside. Attitudes help make us match! When our attitude is good on the inside, it comes out on the outside! For example, if we have a loving attitude, we're going to be kind and say nice things. But if our attitude is sour and mean, we might turn into bullies or say unkind words to others. Let's see what the Bible says about attitudes and how they affect our actions.** Read aloud Proverbs 15:30 and Matthew 23:26b. Then ask:

♥ TIDBITS ♥
This object lesson, with its bright colorful eggs, is perfect around spring-time or Easter!

- ♥ **How do our attitudes affect the way we act positively? negatively?**
- ♥ **What are positive attitudes God wants us to have?**
- ♥ **How can you make sure your attitudes match your actions?**

Form small groups and look at the outsides of the painted eggs. Say: **Your eggs are beautiful on the outside, but do they match on the inside? Let's peek!** Invite kids to gently peel away the shells and hold up their eggs for everyone to admire. Say: **Wow! The beauty of your eggs is on the inside as well as on the outside— and that's just how God wants us to be. When we have happy, helpful attitudes, our actions will match! Let's share a prayer asking God to help us keep our attitudes cheerful and positive so we do kind things for others.** Pray: **Dear God, we know that how we feel on the inside comes out on the outside. Please help us have loving, positive attitudes so we can serve you in love and kindness. Amen.**

Set out the salt shaker and let kids nibble their colorful treats as they discuss ways they can nurture positive attitudes about school, family, friends, church, and serving God. Encourage children to make Happy Attitude Eggs for their families and friends to remind them that positive attitudes are positively pleasing! ♥

Follow the Flock

THE VALUE DU JOUR:
Following God

OOD FOR THOUGHT

We can go for God! (*Leviticus 18:4; Deuteronomy 13:4; 1 John 5:3*)

IMPLE INGREDIENTS

You'll need a Bible, a loaf of sliced wheat or white bread, peanut butter or cheese spread, raisins, maraschino cherry halves, large twisted pretzels, plastic knives, and paper towels.

EVOURING THE MESSAGE

Have kids form pairs and invite partners to take turns playing Follow the Leader, with actions such as tapping tummies, hopping in place, clapping, and so on. Be sure each partner has a chance to lead several actions. Then say: **In games like Follow the Leader or Simon Says, it's pretty easy to follow along. But sometimes when God calls us to follow him, it's not as easy. Abraham found that out when God called him to follow. What did Abraham do when God asked him to leave his home?**

Help kids remember that Abraham took his wife Sarai and their flocks of sheep and goats and bravely followed God. Then say: **When God called Abraham to action, Abraham said, "Let's go!" He trusted God and followed wherever God led. Let's see if you can follow my directions for making a flock of edible goats to remind us how Abraham said, "Let's go!" and followed God.**

While children work in pairs, give directions for making the sandwiches. First, have one partner spread peanut butter or cheese spread on one slice of bread, then have the other partner place a second slice of bread on top and cut the sandwich diagonally to make four triangles. Next, have partners use peanut butter or cheese spread as "glue" to stick on raisin eyes and cherry noses. Finally, show kids how to break three-ring pretzels in half to make goats' horns. As kids work, have them discuss why it's not always easy to follow God but always wise. As kids nibble their goodies, read aloud Leviticus 18:4; Deuteronomy 13:4; and 1 John 5:3. Then ask:

🍎 **Why is it important to follow God when he calls us?**

🍎 **How do trust and faith play a role in following God?**

🍎 **In what ways can we "go for God" today?**

Have kids form a circle and say: **Let's have a Follow the Leader type of prayer. I'll say one thing and do an action, then you repeat and follow me. Ready? Dear God** *(kneel down),* **please help us jump when you call** *(hop up)* **and follow in whatever way you ask of us.** *(March around the room as you continue.)* **Help us turn from things that stop us from following you** *(turn around one time)* **and give us strength** *(flex your muscles)* **to stay by your side. We love you.** *(Blow a kiss upward.)* **Amen.**

Say: **You followed along in our opening game, you followed along in making a flock of tasty treats, and you followed in our prayer. Now let's all get up and go for God—because he's the best leader to follow!** 🍎

Seeing Stars

THE VALUE DU JOUR:

Acceptance

OOD FOR THOUGHT

God knows what's in our hearts. *(1 Samuel 16:7; Galatians 5:22, 23)*

IMPLE INGREDIENTS

You'll need a Bible, sturdy plastic knives, a box of brown sugar, 1/4-cup measuring cups, napkins, one small package of cream cheese for every eight children, paper bowls and spoons, and one apple for every four kids.

Before class, place one-half package of cream cheese in each bowl to soften at room temperature. Wash and dry the apples.

DEVOURING THE MESSAGE

Form groups of four and hold up an apple. Invite kids to describe what they see, such as the apple's red skin, the rounded shape, a stem, or even the apple's shine. Then say: **The things you described were traits from looking at the outside of the apple. But do they really tell us what an apple is like? Do they describe the inside appearance of the apple or how it tastes or even how nutritious an apple is? Just looking at something or someone from the outside doesn't tell us very much. So how should we look at others? Let's see what the Bible says about how God views people.** Read aloud 1 Samuel 16:7, then ask:

🍎 **How does God look at us?**

🍎 **What do you think it means that God looks at our hearts?**

🍎 **Why is it good that God doesn't judge us from our outward appearances?**

Say: **Instead of looking at us from the outside, God looks at the condition of our hearts. In other words, God wants to know us according to how we think and feel instead of what color our hair is or how tall we are. When God looks at the condition of our hearts, he knows us inside and out! Now let's see what's inside these apples.**

Hand an apple, napkins, and a sturdy plastic knife to each group of four kids. Demonstrate how to carefully cut the apples width-wise across the center. (The seeds should make star-shaped patterns.) Point out the star shapes made by the apple seeds, then say: **Look at the lovely stars! Who would have thought stars could be inside apples! That's the way it is when we look inside others. We often find many wonderful surprises. Maybe the neighbor you thought was a bully really has a kind spot inside his heart or the teacher who seems cranky is actually patient and forgiving. Let's finish our treats as we learn more about the way God looks at us.**

Hand each group a spoon and a paper bowl containing softened cream cheese. Put 1/4 cup of brown sugar into the cream cheese and stir it well to make smooth, creamy caramel dip. Show kids how to cut their apple halves into quarters, then dip the apples into the caramel for a great taste treat! As you dip and munch, read aloud Galatians 5:22, 23 and discuss things God wants to see in our hearts and lives, such as kindness, love, forgiveness, and patience.

Say: **God looks at us in a very special way. He knows what's in our hearts, and he understands our deepest feelings and thoughts. We can look at others in the same way so we understand and accept them with compassion. Let's share a prayer asking God to help us look at others in this wonderful way.** Pray: **Dear God, we're glad you look at our hearts instead of our outside appearances. Please help us look at others in this way so we can accept them and be compassionate to them. Amen.**

Encourage kids to make these tasty treats for their families and friends as they show them the apple-stars as reminders that God knows what's in our hearts. 🍎

Upside-Down Delight

THE VALUE DU JOUR:
Relying on God

OOD FOR THOUGHT

We can trust in and rely on God's help. *(Psalm 91:14-16; 1 John 4:16)*

IMPLE INGREDIENTS

You'll need a Bible, vanilla or other flavored ice cream, small paper bowls, plastic spoons, an ice-cream dipper, sugar cones, and small assorted candies, nuts, and raisins. You'll also need pencils and small slips of paper.

Be sure you have a pointed sugar cone for each child. If you can't find this type of cone, use flat-bottomed cones instead.

EVOURING THE MESSAGE

Ask kids to imagine a wonderful ice-cream cone topped with their favorite flavors. Have them shout the flavors out loud, then say: **Now imagine that ice-cream cone falling and turning upside down! Oh, what a** messy situation! Sometimes we feel like that ice-cream cone! We might feel all turned upside down with troubles and feel as though there's no help in sight. Can you think of a time you felt turned around and upside down?

Encourage kids to tell about their experiences, then say: **When we're feeling topsy-turvy, there is someone who will always help. Let's see who it is. Stand up and hang your head over like you're upside down. I'll read a verse from the Bible, and when you know who helps us, pop right side up!** Read aloud Psalm 91:14-16 and 1 John 4:16. Wait for children to respond, then ask:

🍎 **Why do you think God wants to help us when things seem upside down?**

🍎 **How does relying on God keep us right side up and strengthen our faith?**

🍎 **Why is it smarter to trust God rather than worry in messy situations?**

🍎 **Who could you encourage this week by telling him about God's help?**

Explain that you'll be making upside-down clowns as a reminder that even when we feel upside down, God can turn our problems around and make us happy again. Have each child place a scoop of ice cream in a bowl, then add a sugar cone to look like a clown's hat. Stick candies, nuts, and raisins on the ice cream for facial features. (If you would like, provide tube icing so kids can add decorations to the clowns' hats.) As you work, have kids suggest ways that we can ask for and rely on God's help, such as by praying or by confiding in a loving adult or friend. Point out that God often sends others to help us during hard situations.

🍎 **TIDBITS** 🍎

Kids might enjoy knowing that ice-cream bars were invented by Christian Nelson, who combined ice cream and a chocolate candy bar into one shivery treat! He called his new delight the Eskimo Pie.

As kids enjoy their upside-down clowns, say: **It's important to know that God is here to help us when we're feeling turned around and upside down! Because God loves us, he can turn any problem right side up! All we need to do is ask for God's help, then trust in his answers. An upside-down ice-cream cone is usually a mess, but with God keeping us right side up, we will be able to smile like our ice-cream clowns!**

Let's share a prayer thanking God for his special help and asking him to help us rely on his help through any troubles or worries. Pray: **Dear God, thank you for always being ready to help us when troubles and worries make us feel upside down. Please help us to rely on you more each day. Amen.**

End by challenging kids to write down any worries they may have on slips of paper. Have them tape the papers upside down to their bedroom doors or bedposts, then pray for those concerns each night for a week. After a week, remind kids to review the papers and when a problem has been resolved, to turn the paper right side up and give God a big, happy "thank you!" 🍎

All Shook Up!

OOD FOR THOUGHT

Patience and perseverance strengthen faith! *(Proverbs 19:11; James 1:2-4, 12)*

IMPLE INGREDIENTS

You'll need a Bible, two plastic jars with tight lids, two plastic bowls, two pints of whole whipping cream, honey, plastic knives, and sliced bread.

EVOURING THE MESSAGE

In this shake-em-up snack idea, you'll be shaking jars of whipping cream firmly for about ten minutes, but don't give up! The cream will eventually separate into a lump of sweet butter!

Pour a pint of whipping cream into each container and place the lids on securely. Have children sit in a circle and give each child several moments to shake the contents firmly. Have kids continue shaking and passing the jars as you say: **Patience and perseverance are often hard to have. It can be hard to wait for a birthday or a vacation or a special visit from Grandma and Grandpa. When was a time you were impatient?**

Allow kids to share their experiences, then say: **There are many times when patience and perseverance can help us keep going or trying. Just like now, you're persevering by shaking these jars over and over—and being patient to see what happens. That's how it is with faith in God. It sometimes feels as if all we do is wait for God to answer prayers or work in our lives. But what happens if we give up?** Have

> ♥ TIDBITS ♥
> *Kids might enjoy learning that bread wasn't sold sliced and in plastic packages until 1928, an innovation that prompted the saying, "It's the best thing since sliced bread!"*

kids stop shaking the jars for a moment. **Giving up stops things from happening! If we lose patience and give up, nothing will develop!**

Have children begin shaking and passing the jars again as you read aloud Proverbs 19:11a and James 1:2-4, 12. Then ask:

🍎 **How do patience and perseverance affect our faith?**

🍎 **Why do you think God wants us to be patient? to persevere?**

🍎 **What is one thing you could be more patient with? How can God help you?**

By now the cream should be separated into a lump in each jar. Explain that the lump is butter and the liquid is called buttermilk. Carefully remove the lumps of butter from each jar and place them in bowls. Drizzle honey over the butter, then invite kids to spread this delicious treat on sliced bread. Say: **Patience and perseverance are two sweet values to generously spread throughout our lives! Let's ask for God's help in being more patient and persevering and to trust God's timing!** Pray: **Dear God, please help us be more patient and persevering with the people we meet, in our faith toward you, and in all we do! Amen.**

Consider having your kids present this object lesson to a younger class. Invite the younger children to get shakin' as they learn about patience, perseverance, and trusting God's timing in a delicious way! 🍎

Edible Ant Farm

THE VALUE DU JOUR:
Cooperation

OOD FOR THOUGHT

Cooperation gets things done! *(Galatians 6:2; 3 John 5)*

IMPLE INGREDIENTS

You'll need a Bible, plastic resealable sandwich bags, graham crackers, chocolate cake sprinkles, a large plastic bowl, a rolling pin, waxed paper, and plastic spoons.

DEVOURING THE MESSAGE

Cover a table with waxed paper and set the items out in this order: the graham crackers and rolling pin, the large bowl, plastic spoons and sandwich bags, and chocolate cake sprinkles.

Ask a volunteer to lie on the floor and another child to try and pick up the volunteer. Keep adding kids to the lifting process until the volunteer is hoisted a few inches off the ground. Carefully set the volunteer down and ask why it was easier to pick someone up when lots of people cooperated.

Say: **Cooperation and helping one another is the best way to get things done! Did you know that even God's tiniest creatures cooperate with one another? Ants live in colonies and work together to gather food, build their tunnels, and care for their young. Every ant has its own special job and way to help! In God's kingdom, we each have our own special places and ways to help, too. And when we cooperate, we can do many wonderful things for God! Let's cooperatively make a neat snack, then learn more about this important value and how we can be more cooperative with others.**

Have children form an assembly line and assign two or three kids to crush graham crackers using the rolling pin. The next group of kids will scoop the crumbs into the large bowl. Another group will fill the sandwich bags half full, and the last group can add a small spoonful of chocolate cake sprinkle "ants" to each bag. As children work, make comments such as "I like the way you're help-ing each other" and "See what cooperation can accomplish?"

When all the bags have been cooperatively assembled, hand each child a bag and a plastic spoon so kids can nibble their Edible Ant Farms! As children enjoy their snacks, read aloud Galatians 6:2 and 3 John 5. Then ask:

🍎 **Why is cooperation important in church? with our families? at school?**

🍎 **What might happen if we're not cooperative and helpful?**

🍎 **How can we cooperate more with God? with others?**

🍎 **What great things can cooperating accomplish in our lives? in our com-munity? in the world?**

Say: **Even ants know the value of cooperation! They know that one or two can be a help, but many who cooperate can build a mountain! Just think what we can do for God if we all cooperate and serve him at once!**

Close with a prayer thanking God for Christians who cooperate in serving God together. Consider a cooperative service project such as making Edible Ant Farms to give to patients in a children's hospital or kids in a homeless shelter. Tape to the bags cheery cards with Galatians 6:2 written on them. 🍎

Can't-Hide Pitas

THE VALUE DU JOUR:
Honesty

OOD FOR THOUGHT

We want to be open and honest with God. *(Psalm 139:1-4; Proverbs 12:22)*

IMPLE INGREDIENTS

You'll need a Bible, pita-pocket bread, paper towels, Life Savers, lettuce, fish-shaped crackers, shredded cheese, and Italian salad dressing.

Before class, be sure you have a pita pocket for each child. If you want smaller snacks, cut the pitas in half.

EVOURING THE MESSAGE

Set up a table with the food in assembly-line order: first the Life Savers, then the pita pockets, the lettuce, the shredded cheese, the fish-shaped crackers, the salad dressing, and, finally, the paper towels.

Gather kids and say: **We've all tried to hide something. Maybe it was a surprise birthday gift, a secret, or the truth. Maybe you even tried to hide yourself in a game of Hide-and-Seek. The Bible tells us about Jonah and how he tried to hide from God—only this wasn't a game! God wanted Jonah to go to Nineveh and tell the people to obey God. But Jonah was scared and tried to hide from God. First he hid on a boat, then was tossed into the sea! Let's make hidden Jonah snacks as I tell you the rest of the story about hide-n-seek Jonah and how he learned you can't hide from God!**

Hand each child a pita pocket and a Life Savers (Jonah). Have kids assemble their pita pockets as you tell the following story: **Jonah fell down into the sea, but along came a giant fish and swallowed Jonah up!** *Have kids drop their candy into the pita pocket "fish."* **Jonah was so afraid! Here he was inside the** belly of a giant fish! And just look at all the stuff that fish had swallowed! There was lots of seaweed *(add lettuce to the pita pocket)* and **fish** *(sprinkle fish-shaped crackers on the lettuce)*, **long, slithery eels** *(add shredded cheese)* **and lots and lots of seawater!** *(Shake Italian salad dressing over the salad mix.)*

But where was Jonah in all this? Deep inside the fish's tummy praying! Jonah knew he had been wrong to disobey God and to try to hide from him. So Jonah prayed and told God he was sorry. For three days and nights Jonah prayed inside that big fish! And God heard his prayers. On the third day, God made the fish spit Jonah out on the sand. And Jonah promptly obeyed God and ran to Nineveh to warn the people to change their ways and be more obedient to God! Yeah, Jonah!

Give each child a paper towel. Then invite kids to sit in a circle and munch their pita-pocket fish, keeping an eye out for Jonah. Tell them to set their candy Jonahs aside when they're found. Read aloud Psalm 139:1-4 and Proverbs 12:22 and ask:

🍂 Why is it important to be open and not hide from God?

🍂 Why is it good to be honest with God in our words as well as our actions? honest with others in word and deed?

🍂 In what ways does being honest with God help us be honest with others?

🍂 How does honesty to God show our love? our respect? our faith?

After the pita fish are gobbled up and the candy Jonahs collected, say: **Hold your candy Jonah up and peek through the hole. Just as we can see clearly through these holes, God can see everything we do. When we're open and honest with God, we never need to hide from him, his help, or his love!** Let's share a prayer and ask God to help us be open and honest at all times with him and with others. When we say "amen," pop the candy Jonah into your mouth to remind you what a lifesaver God is when we keep our eyes on him! Pray: **Dear God, we're glad you know where we are and what we're thinking at all times. Please help us be open and honest with you and others in all we say and do. We love you, God! Amen.**

Encourage children to make these yummy treats for their families and friends as a reminder that God knows everything about us, so we never have to hide from him! 🍂

🍂 **TIDBITS** 🍂

Life Savers were invented by mistake when candy maker Clarence Crane wanted small, flat mints but his machine punched holes in the center. They reminded him of life preservers, but they can remind us of Jonah's miraculous lifesaver—God!

Monster Munchies

OOD FOR THOUGHT

We're humble beside the Creator. *(Deuteronomy 4:32; Isaiah 40:28; Ephesians 4:2)*

IMPLE INGREDIENTS

You'll need a Bible, paper plates, toothpicks, and fresh fruits and vegetables, including carrots, celery, apples, cucumbers, grapes, potatoes, yams, and olives. You'll need one apple for each child.

Before class, chop and cut all the fruits and vegetables except the apples into interesting shapes and pieces. Kids will use toothpicks to attach foods to their apples to make funny sculptures.

EVOURING THE MESSAGE

Place the food items, paper plates, and toothpicks on the table, then hand each child an apple. Say: **Look at the lovely apples you're holding. Although people took care of these apples in an orchard, they didn't create the apples or the trees on which the apples grew. But people can make things from apples. What are some of the wonderful things to do with apples?** Allow kids to tell their ideas, which might include apple pie, applesauce, fried apples, caramel apples, or even dried apple crafts.

Then ask kids who created the apples and apple trees. Say: **God created all things on and under and above the earth. And only God is the Creator. We may be able to make things, but only God can truly create! It makes us feel humble to know that all we make and do pale compared to what God creates and has created! Humility means standing in awe of God and knowing that God is so much bigger than we are—and so much more powerful! Let's listen to all that**

God has done! Ask several volunteers to read aloud Deuteronomy 4:32; Isaiah 40:28; and Ephesians 4:2. Then ask:

- 🍎 **How does it feel to know that only God creates and that we just make things?**
- 🍎 **Why is it good that God, and not people, created the world?**
- 🍎 **Why is having a humble attitude important in praising God?**
- 🍎 **In what ways can we give God the glory for all of creation?**

Then invite kids to make funny monster food sculptures, using the apples as heads or bodies and the cut fruits and vegetables as facial features. Attach the food bits with toothpicks. While kids work, say: **Your munchy monsters are so cute! You're doing a good job of making them. It's fun to make things we can be proud of, but we must remain humble knowing that God is the only true Creator!**

When the Monster Munchies are complete, invite children to take turns showing what they made. Then munch the goodies as you visit about your favorite parts of God's creation. End with a closing prayer thanking God for being the Creator and asking for God's help in remaining humble and in giving praise and glory to God for all he does. 🍎

Fluffy Truffle Sheep

THE VALUE DU JOUR:
Nearness to God

OOD FOR THOUGHT

Staying close to God is important. *(Psalm 73:28; Luke 15:3-7; James 4:8)*

IMPLE INGREDIENTS

You'll need a Bible, powdered sugar, peanut butter, a small bowl of honey, plastic spoons, cupcake liners, and small bowls of shredded coconut, chocolate sprinkles, and powdered cocoa.

Before class, make edible dough by thoroughly mixing 2 cups of powdered sugar and 1/3 cup of peanut butter. Cream the ingredients together until very smooth and dough-like. If the mixture is too sticky, add more powdered sugar; if it's too dry, add more peanut butter or a few drops of water. Store in an airtight container until ready for your object lesson. The dough will store up to three days.

DEVOURING THE MESSAGE

Gather kids and ask them to describe times they may have been lost or wandered away from someone in a store. Encourage them to express what it was like being lost and how it felt to be found. Then say: **Being lost can be scary. It feels unfamiliar and maybe even unsafe. When we wander away from a parent or become lost in a store, we want more than anything to be found! Did you know there are ways to wander away from God? What do you think those ways might be?** Allow time for children to share their thoughts, which might include not obeying God, not reading the Bible, not praying, or doing mean things to others.

After children have shared their ideas, say: **We are like sheep in God's flock, and when one of us wanders away, God is very unhappy and wants us found. Because God loves us, he wants us to stay close to him at all times. Let's listen to a biblical story about a lost sheep as we make Fluffy Truffle Sheep to munch and enjoy.**

Read aloud Luke 15:3-7 as you show kids how to make sheep truffles. Have each child take a portion of candy dough and roll it into a ball about the size of a walnut. Use a plastic spoon to dip the ball into the bowl of honey, then roll the "sheep" in coconut, chocolate sprinkles, or powdered cocoa, depending on what color and texture of sheep you'd like. Place the finished sheep in cupcake liners.

When the story is finished, have children set their sheep on the floor or table in front of them. Ask:

🍎 **Why is it important to stay close to God?**

🍎 **How can staying close to God help us have faith? be strong? be loving?**

🍎 **In what ways can we be close to God every day?**

Say: **Just as sheep stay close to their shepherd, we want to stay close to God. Jesus used the story we just heard to explain that God wants us near and will find us if we wander away. But we have to be willing to remain close to God at all times. Remember, God never wanders away from us—it's we who sometimes wander! Before we nibble our candy sheep, let's share a prayer thanking God for his love and asking his help in staying close to him.** Pray: **Dear Lord, thank you for loving us and wanting us near. We want to stay close to you in all we say and do. That's because we love you, too! Amen.**

As kids enjoy their treats, read aloud Psalm 73:28 and James 4:8. Then invite children to share ways we can grow closer to God in the things we do and in what we say. Encourage kids to name examples, such as learning God's Word, praying every day, doing kind things for others, and encouraging others with kind words. 🍎

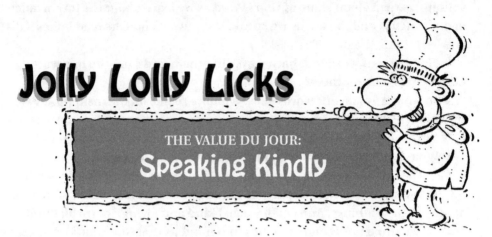

Jolly Lolly Licks

THE VALUE DU JOUR:
Speaking Kindly

OOD FOR THOUGHT

We want to speak kindly. *(Psalm 145:21; James 3:8-10)*

IMPLE INGREDIENTS

You'll need a Bible, new craft sticks, waxed paper, powdered sugar, butter or margarine, red food coloring, and pink cake sprinkles.

Before class, prepare edible dough by mixing a box of powdered sugar with 3 tablespoons melted butter and several drops of red food coloring. Mix and knead the pink dough until it's thick and stiff enough to hold its shape once molded. If the dough is too dry, add a bit more butter. If the dough is too sticky, add more powdered sugar. Store the dough in an airtight container until you need it. This dough will last several days.

EVOURING THE MESSAGE

Set out the dough, candy sprinkles, and craft sticks. Spread wax paper where kids will be working. Gather children and say: **I have a funny riddle for you. See if you can guess what I'm talking about.**

It's with each of us throughout our days.

It's not sharp like a knife but can cut both ways.

What is it?

Allow children to tell their ideas, then say: **Let me give you a clue. It's the last place our words are before they reach someone's ears! I was describing our** tongues! Wiggle your tongue so we can be sure you all have one! You know, the Bible says some very important things about our tongues. Let's have several volunteers read aloud some of God's Word as we learn about the importance of our tongues and the words we speak. Have two volunteers read James 3:8-10 and Psalm 145:21 aloud. Then ask:

🍎 How can our words cut both ways? In other words, how do our words both help and hurt others?

🍎 In what ways do our words show what we're like on the inside? how we think and feel?

🍎 Why should we be careful of what words come out on our tongues?

🍎 What kinds of words do you think God wants us to speak?

Say: The Bible tells us we should tame our tongues—but it's really what is in our hearts and our minds that needs taming! When we feel mean, we're more apt to say mean things. And when we feel kind and loving, we speak kindly! Let's make some nifty candy tongues to remind us that God wants us to speak sweet words of kindness and encouragement to others.

Hand each child a craft stick and a golf-ball-sized lump of dough. Show kids how to fashion tongues from the dough. Be sure the candy tongues are at least 1/2-inch thick at the base.
Poke the sticks through the base of the candy tongues, then sprinkle candy "taste buds" over the tops of the tongues. (You may need to gently push the candy taste buds onto the treats.)

After the snacks are made, say: Let's use our candy tongues—and our real tongues—to offer a prayer asking God to help us speak sweet words at all times. When you hear me say a sweet word, repeat that word and then take one lick of your treat. Pray: Dear God, you are wonderful. *(Pause for responses.)* Thank you for giving us kind words to say. *(Pause.)* Please help us remember to speak sweet words instead of mean ones. *(Pause.)* Help us speak words that encourage, lift, and help others *(pause)*—and words to praise you, too! *(Pause.)* Amen.

As children finish their clever treats, encourage them to mill around and speak kind and encouraging words to their classmates. Challenge them to speak to each person and say at least one kind thing to every person they meet. 🍎

Banana Sparklers

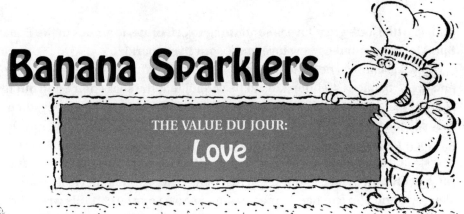

THE VALUE DU JOUR:

Love

OOD FOR THOUGHT

Let's celebrate a life of love! *(1 Corinthians 13:4-7, 13; 1 John 4:19)*

IMPLE INGREDIENTS

You'll need a Bible, a bowl of honey, colorful cake sprinkles, paper plates, a banana for each child, new craft sticks, newsprint, a marker, and tape.

EVOURING THE MESSAGE

Place the food items and supplies on a table and gather kids. Tape a piece of newsprint to the wall, then challenge kids to brainstorm all the emotions they can think of as you write them down. Suggestions might include anger, surprise, love, joy, irritation, frustration, happiness, puzzlement, boredom, excitement, and so on. Next, ask kids to rate the emotions as either negative (such as anger and jealousy) or positive (such as kindness and love). Finally, ask kids which emotion they'd choose to have all the time and why.

Say: **Every day we have a new chance to choose the way we're going to feel and behave. Positive emotions are good and productive because they help others and keep us happy. But which emotion is the best of the positives? Let's see what the Bible says. Put your hands on your hearts when you know!** Read aloud 1 Corinthians 13:4-7, 13 and 1 John 4:19. Then ask:

🌱 **Why do you think love is the greatest emotion we can feel?**

🌱 **What good things happen when we're filled with God's love?**

🌱 **How does a loving attitude affect how we treat others? respond to God?**

🌱 **In what ways can we spread a loving attitude to others so they can celebrate a more loving lifestyle?**

Hand each child a craft stick, a banana, and a paper plate. Say: **Choosing to live with a loving attitude and heart is something to celebrate. And knowing** we live with God's great love is something to celebrate, too. Let's make Banana Sparklers to remind us how love makes our lives sparkle!

Show kids how to peel their bananas and poke craft sticks up through one end of the bananas. Caution kids to be careful that the sticks don't pop out the sides of the bananas! Have kids lightly roll or dip the bananas in honey, then sprinkle the fruit with the sparkly sprinkles.

When the Banana Sparklers are ready, form a circle and say: **Before we enjoy our special treats, let's share a prayer and thank God for his gift of love and the celebration of love in our lives. Just before we say "amen," we'll go around the circle and you can name one person to show your love to this week.** Pray: **Dear Lord, thank you for your wondrous gift of love. Please help us choose to have a more loving attitude each day. Help us begin this week by showing love to** (fill in the blank as you go around the circle). **Amen.**

Consider making these special treats as a loving service project for the elderly in a nearby care facility. After kids sprinkle the bananas, slip them into plastic sandwich bags and tie ribbons around the craft sticks to seal the bags. Place the bananas in the freezer until they're frozen, then distribute the goodies along with a card expressing your kids' love to God and others! 🍎

Heavenly Haroset

THE VALUE DU JOUR:
Trust

ᖴOOD FOR THOUGHT
We can trust God to help care for us. (Exodus 12:31-34; Psalm 91:9, 10)

ᔕIMPLE INGREDIENTS
You'll need a Bible, water, 1/4 cup of orange juice, a cup of chopped walnuts, 1/4 teaspoon of cinnamon, a bowl and spoon, plastic knives, matzo crackers, and a pound of chopped, pitted dates.

Before class, boil the dates in 1 1/2 cups of water for approximately ten minutes, then drain the water.

EVOURING THE MESSAGE

Gather kids and explain that Passover has been celebrated for centuries by the Israelites (and today by many churches) to remember God's saving grace. Remind kids that during the first Passover night, God protected his people from death in Egypt and that the day after this amazing Passover, the Israelite slaves were set free from Pharaoh's cruel captivity.

Then say: **God's saving power is perfect and strong. God loved the Israelites and knew they needed his power and protection. So God caused Pharaoh to set the Israelites free! And because God loves us, we can trust that he will help us and care for us, too. By trusting in God's help and love, we can be set free from worries, troubles, and sadness.**

When Passover is celebrated, two of the foods eaten are matzo bread and haroset, a fruit paste to spread on the matzo. Let's make this tasty treat to remind us of God's saving grace and power and of our need to trust God to set us free.

Have kids help mix the dates, orange juice, chopped walnuts, and cinnamon in a bowl. Let each child take a turn adding an ingredient or stirring the mixture. As children prepare the haroset, read aloud Exodus 12:31-34. Then explain that the Israelites' faith in God's grace was shown as they hurriedly prepared the matzo, which didn't have time to rise before they fled Egypt. Explain that haroset was to remind the Israelites of the mortar they made to prepare bricks for Pharaoh when they were slaves.

♥ TIDBITS ♥
Here's a fun devotion for Passover! Kids might enjoy knowing that matzo (or matza shmuraa) is a type of unleavened bread that must be prepared in less than eighteen minutes to prevent any rising of the dough.

When the haroset is finished, let children spread the treat on the matzo crackers. Then ask:

- ♥ Why can we trust God to help care for us?
- ♥ In what ways is God's help a demonstration of his love?
- ♥ How does trusting God help us in times of trouble? help us live more bravely?
- ♥ How can you show God you trust him this week?

Say: **Our mini Passover celebration is a delicious quick snack. But knowing we have God's love and help in our lives makes us want to celebrate every day, all day! Let's close with a prayer thanking God that we can live happily and securely as we trust God's help and loving care.** Pray: **Dear God, thank you for**

your never-ending love and saving grace. It's so good to know we can trust you to help and care for us! Amen.** End by reading aloud Psalm 91:9, 10.

Consider making this special treat for another children's class or an adult Sunday school class. Invite your guests to a Passover party and read aloud Exodus 12:31-34. Have kids remind everyone that we can trust God's love to help us live more freely and securely. End by having your guests form a circle and pray for God to answer and help each need in every person's heart. 🍎

Commandment Pops

THE VALUE DU JOUR:
Obedience

OOD FOR THOUGHT

Obeying God is always wise. *(Deuteronomy 5:7-21; 6:24; 1 John 5:3)*

IMPLE INGREDIENTS

You'll need a Bible, a box of graham crackers, paper towels, a bowl of icing, plastic knives, new craft sticks, and a bowl of granola or crushed peanuts.

Before class, make sure you have two whole graham crackers for each child plus several extras in case of breakage.

EVOURING THE MESSAGE

Gather kids and ask them to tell about rules they may have at home or at school. Encourage them to tell why these rules were made and why they should be obeyed.

Then say: **Rules are made to keep us safe and happy—and they're made to be obeyed. Some rules are important, while others may be life-saving,**

such as rules around a swimming
important rules for us to obey are Go
up Mount Sinai and talked with God? G
ing. We call these rules the Ten Commands. But the very most
Moses on two stone tablets.   her when Moses went

Hand each child two graham crackers, a new special rules for liv-
Continue: **God used his finger to write these im**ave these rules to
the tablets, then he gave them to Moses to take to
the rest of the story, use your sticks to carefully carvoaper towel.
graham-cracker tablet and the word "obey" on the othuents on

As kids carve their edible tablets, say: **God put ten comm**.As I tell
tablets. What did they say? Let's read the Ten Commandmen one
Read aloud Deuteronomy 5:7-21. Then ask:

- ❦ **Why did God give us rules to live by?**
- ❦ **How do God's commandments demonstrate his love for us?**
- ❦ **How does obedience show our faith in God? our love for him?**
- ❦ **Why is it wise to obey God?**

When the graham-cracker tablets are carved, show kids how to spread i
on the sides of the crackers without writing on them, then sandwich their cra
sticks between the graham crackers to make
commandments-on-a-stick. Finally, "glue"
granola (or peanut) pebbles to the graham-
cracker tablets by spreading a line of icing
across the top and bottom of each cracker,
then sticking granola to the sweet stuff.

Before nibbling the stone tablets, read
aloud Deuteronomy 6:24 and 1 John 5:3. Then say: **Let's thank God for giving us
such loving and important rules and ask God's help in being obedient to him
all through our lives. Hold your Commandment Pop close to your heart as we
pray.** Pray: **Dear God, thank you for giving us your commandments to follow
and obey. Your commandments show your love for us, and because we love
you, we want to obey them. Please help us be more obedient in all we say and
do. Amen.**

As kids munch and crunch their edible tablets, review the Ten Commandments
once more and see if kids can remember the order of God's special rules. (If
there's time, list the Ten Commandments on a sheet of newsprint and work to
memorize them over the next few weeks.) ❦

Chips

Scr...
U JOUR:
...eachable

THOUGHT

...ep learning God's Word. *(Psalm 119:105; 2 Timothy*

...PLE INGREDIENTS

You'll need a Bible, a bag of regular potato chips, waxed paper, plastic forks, a bowl of melted milk chocolate, cookie sheets, and photocopies of the Scripture strips on page 29.

Before class, melt the chocolate chips in a microwave or a fondue pot. Kids will be dipping potato chips in the chocolate, then setting them on waxed paper to harden. You may need to thin the chocolate with a bit of water if it's too thick. Access to a freezer is helpful in hardening the dipped chips, but if you'd rather not use chocolate or don't have time for a freezer, simply substitute colorful tube icing to drizzle on the chips. Photocopy the Scripture strips from page 29 and cut them out. You'll need two strips for each child. Finally, cover several cookie sheets with waxed paper.

DEVOURING THE MESSAGE

Set out the waxed paper, plastic forks, melted chocolate, potato chips, and the Scripture strips. Gather children and invite them to tell about things they've learned since they were babies. Suggestions might include learning to walk and talk, to read, or to ride a bike.

Say: **There are so many important things we learn when we're young! They are all things we need to know to function in the world and be happy. Just think how hard it would be if we hadn't learned to communicate or read! Some people think that when we're older, we don't need to learn as much as when we're young. But** that's not true! We want to have a spirit of being teachable all our lives, especially when it comes to God's Word! What does the Bible say about learning God's Word? Let's see! Read aloud Psalm 119:105 and 2 Timothy 3:16, 17; 4:2. Then ask:

- 🍎 Why is it important to learn and understand what God says?
- 🍎 How can learning God's Word help us? draw us closer to God?
- 🍎 What are ways we can learn more about God and his Word?

Say: **Learning is an ongoing process. We want to be open to learn things our whole lives long—especially God's Word! Let's make some cool treats as we exercise our spirit of learning!**

Have each child choose two Scripture strips and fold them into small rectangles. Then direct everyone to choose two folded-over potato chips—the kind that look a bit like tacos. Have kids slide the Scripture strips inside, then hook plastic fork tines into the open ends of the chips. Demonstrate how to use another fork to carefully drizzle chocolate over the outside of the chips, being careful not to let the chocolate drip on the paper strips. Carefully lay the choco-chips on the cookie sheets and place them in the freezer for half an hour. (If you choose to use tube icing instead of chocolate, there's no need for freezing.)

After the chips are chilled and the chocolate has hardened, have children choose two chips to nibble. Let them remove the Scripture verses and take turns reading them aloud. Challenge the kids to work at learning their two verses during the coming week. Then see who can repeat the Scripture verses the next time you meet. Close with the following prayer: **Dear God, thank you for your Word and all its love and wisdom. Please help us be teachable and look for new ways to learn about you! Amen.** 🍎

Your word is a lamp to my feet and a light for my path.
(Psalm 119:105)

- -

All Scripture is God-breathed and is useful for teaching, rebuking, correcting and training in righteousness.
(2 Timothy 3:16)

- -

Your word is a lamp to my feet and a light for my path.
(Psalm 119:105)

- -

All Scripture is God-breathed and is useful for teaching, rebuking, correcting and training in righteousness.
(2 Timothy 3:16)

Good Fruit Salads

THE VALUE DU JOUR:
Fruit of the Spirit

OOD FOR THOUGHT

God wants us to develop spiritual fruit in our lives. *(Galatians 5:22, 23; Ephesians 5:18)*

IMPLE INGREDIENTS

You'll need a Bible, black permanent markers, maraschino cherries, apple and banana bits, grapes, plastic spoons, and an orange for each child.

Before class, cut the tops from the oranges and hollow out the fruit and juice. Save the orange pieces and juice for the recipe.

EVOURING THE MESSAGE

Set out the fruits, markers, plastic spoons, and orange bowls. Gather kids and ask if they have any talents they'd like to briefly tell about or demonstrate. Encourage everyone to participate.

Then say: **Everyone has different talents and gifts. That's what makes each of us unique! Some people are super singers or painters; others are math whizzes or awesome athletes. God has given each of us many talents that we can use to serve him. But did you know God also has certain qualities that he wants all of us to have? The Bible calls these qualities the fruit of the Spirit because the Holy Spirit helps us have them in our lives. Listen to the different things that God wants to give us in our lives.** Read aloud Galatians 5:22, 23. Then ask:

🍎 **Why do you think the Bible calls these the "fruit" of the Spirit?**

🍎 **Which of these qualities is easiest for you to show to others?**

🍎 **How could you use this fruit to serve God? to help others?**

🍎 **Which of these qualities is hardest for you to show? Why?**

🍎 **What could you do to develop this quality more in your life?**

Say: **As we finish learning more about the fruit of the Spirit and how we can use these wonderful gifts to serve God and others, let's make cool-n-fruity Good Fruit Salads. Choose different fruits to go into your orange bowls, then draw a face on your bowl to show how it feels to serve God with the fruit of the Spirit.**

As kids assemble their fruit salads, briefly discuss each element of the fruit of the Spirit and how it can help others. When all the fruit bowls are complete, gather kids in a circle and have them hold their salads and think about the different qualities that make up the fruit of the Spirit. Then pray: **Dear Lord, we thank you for giving us special gifts we can use to help others and to serve you. Please help us develop the entire fruit of the Spirit so we can live in a way that pleases you. Amen.**

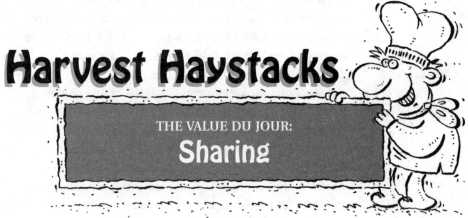

When kids finish eating, read aloud Ephesians 5:18b and encourage kids to fill their lives with the fruit of God's Spirit, just as they filled the bowls with various fruits. Have kids take home the orange cups to dry and harden for several days. 🍎

Harvest Haystacks

THE VALUE DU JOUR:
Sharing

OOD FOR THOUGHT

We can share our blessings from God. *(Romans 12:8; Hebrews 13:16)*

IMPLE INGREDIENTS

You'll need a Bible, a bag of butterscotch chips, two bags of chow mein noodles, cookie sheets, cupcake liners, a mixing bowl, and plastic spoons.

Before class, melt butterscotch chips in a microwave or double boiler. If you have time, consider placing the finished haystacks in the freezer for half an hour to make then shivery cold! Although the haystacks are delicious cold, they're just as tasty without chilling!

DEVOURING THE MESSAGE

Set out the bowl with melted butterscotch chips, the chow mein noodles, plastic spoons, cupcake liners, and cookie sheets. Gather kids and ask them to tell about times they have shared their time or talents. Examples might include sharing toys, giving donations to a food bank, raking leaves for someone, or donating a pencil to a classmate. Encourage kids to tell how it felt to share something they had or could do for someone.

Then say: **Sharing and generosity are wonderful values to have in our lives. Sharing demonstrates our love for others and for God. And with all the blessings God gives each of us every day, we can give to others and spread that generosity. When we share and give, we become God's blessings to others! In Bible times, the harvest was a great time of blessing. Food was collected and a portion set aside to give to God. But God didn't want the sharing to stop there! God wants us to share our blessings with other people, too. As we learn more about giving through God's blessings, let's make Harvest Haystacks to share and enjoy.**

Show children how to gently stir the chow mein noodles into the melted butterscotch, then drop small spoonfuls of the mixture into the cupcake liners. Be sure each child makes three haystacks—one to eat and two to share. Place the liners on cookie sheets and set in the freezer for half an hour—or use the plastic spoons to eat them soft and melty right now! As kids savor their snacks, read aloud Romans 12:8 and Hebrews 13:16. Then ask:

🍎 Why is it important to spread our blessings to others?

🍎 How does sharing demonstrate love for God? others?

🍎 What are ways we can share with others through our time, talents, gifts, and donations?

🍎 Who is someone you can share with in the coming week? How will you share with that person?

Say: **Harvesttime is a good time to share God's blessings, and it's natural during the celebration of Thanksgiving! But we need to live a giving life-**

🍎 **TIDBITS** 🍎

This devotion is perfect for autumn or Thanksgiving! There were five main crop harvests in Jesus' day: flax (Mar.–Apr.), barley (Apr.–May), wheat (May–June), figs and grapes (Aug.–Sept.), and olives (Sept.–Nov.).

style all year long and look for ways to give of ourselves, our time, and our talents. Remember, God doesn't bless us just one time a year! Let's end with a prayer asking God to help us look for ways to share. Pray: **Dear God, we thank you for all the blessings you give us every day. Please help us live a life of giving and generosity so others will see your love! Amen.**

Decide whom you'd like to give your extra haystacks to, such as the minister, an adult Sunday school class, the youth group, or a neighbor of the church. Then present your Harvest Haystacks along with a card reminding the recipient of the sweetness of giving and sharing God's love! (Hebrews 13:16 is an excellent verse to include on the card.) 🍎

No-Bake Hope Cake

THE VALUE DU JOUR:
Hope

OOD FOR THOUGHT

We can have hope because God loves us! *(Psalm 25:4-6; Jeremiah 29:11)*

IMPLE INGREDIENTS

You'll need a Bible, corn syrup, raisins and other dried fruits, powdered cocoa, shredded coconut, plastic spoons, a round cake pan, disposable bowls or large paper cups, and a variety of crunchy cereals.

Before class, be sure the dried fruits are chopped into tiny pieces. This no-bake cake is wonderful if you can refrigerate or freeze it for half an hour, but it will be just as delicious spooned into paper cups without being chilled!

EVOURING THE MESSAGE

Set all the ingredients on a table. Gather kids around the table and hand each child a paper bowl and plastic spoon.

Say: **Many different happy and sad situations are tossed at us during our lives. Tests in school, happy birthdays, sad illnesses, and much more all come our way. As we chat, we'll be making a fun new cake with lots of different things thrown in—just like life! What are some things that happened to you in the last week?**

Encourage kids to share their experiences as they spoon different ingredients into their paper bowls. As you chat, have kids add lots of different ingredients to their bowls until they are one-half to three-fourths full. Save the corn syrup for last.

When the bowls are partially filled, say: **With all the things that are tossed and mixed into our lives, we don't always know which ones will be good and which might not be so great. Just as we're mixing lots of different ingredients together in our bowls, life gives us different ingredients. But even with so many good and bad things happening in our lives, we don't have to worry. We can have hope because of God! We know that because God loves us, he will pour sweet hope for good things over all our lives!**

Pour a half spoonful of corn syrup into each bowl and have kids mix the syrup into the other ingredients. As kids mix their treats, discuss the sweet things God brings to our lives, including hope, love, trust, help, and truth.

Next, have children pour the contents of their bowls into the cake pan. As you pat down the mixture, say: **Wow! What do you think this will taste like? So many things are mixed together!** Chill the cake for half an hour, then finish this devotion. (Or continue from here without chilling the cake.) Say: **Hope means we can joyously trust God to be with us and to make our lives sweeter and better. Let's see what the Bible tells us about having hope.** Read aloud Psalm 25:4-6 and Jeremiah 29:11, then ask:

🍏 **Why is it important to be hopeful?**

🍏 **How does hope help us be braver? closer to God? more worry-free?**

🍏 **How can we inspire God's hope in others to encourage them?**

Spoon the chilled (or unchilled) cake into kids' paper bowls and invite them to crunch the sweet treat. Say: **Our hope cake turned out delicious, didn't it? When we place our hope in God and in his love, all the ingredients in our lives will be sweeter! Let's end with a prayer thanking God that we can live in his hope to make our lives sweeter.** Pray: **Dear God, we're so glad we have hope because of your love! Hope makes the ups and downs of life sweeter and easier to swallow. Help us always remember that we have hope and that our hope is in you! Amen.**

If there's time, let kids write the word "hope" in big letters down the side of a page. Use the H to write the word "heavenly," the O to write "optimism," the P to write "peace," and the E to write "eternally." Explain that hope means we have "heavenly optimism and peace eternally" when our hope is in God. Yes! 🍏

Perfect Peanuts

THE VALUE DU JOUR:
Uniqueness

ᴳOOD FOR THOUGHT

Each of us is special to God! *(John 3:16; 1 John 3:1)*

ˢIMPLE INGREDIENTS

You'll need a Bible, peanuts in the shell, peanut butter, rice cakes, granola, raisins, napkins, and plastic knives. (If you'd like, cut out one blue ribbon for each child and provide markers with which to write on the ribbons.)

ᴰEVOURING THE MESSAGE

Place the ingredients on a table. Have kids form small groups of three or four and hand each group a handful of peanuts in the shell. Direct group members to find the most perfect peanut shell and set the peanut aside. Then have kids open the other peanuts and choose the most perfect peanut from inside the shells. When you're done, ask kids why they chose the peanuts they did.

Say: **It's fun trying to find the perfect peanut, and some really could win blue ribbons, couldn't they? But did you know that God never tries to choose a perfect peanut among us? God loves and values each of us in many unique ways. Even when we make mistakes or do wrong things, God loves us. In other words, we're all special to God and can live with the security of knowing his love for us won't falter, fail, or fade away! Isn't that wonderful? In fact, God loves us and treasures us so much that he sent Jesus to save us from sin and death. Wow! Now that's being special—and uniquely loved! Let's learn more about God's special love for each of us.** Read aloud John 3:16 and 1 John 3:1. Then ask:

* 🌷 **Why do you think God loves each one of us equally but uniquely?**
* 🌷 **In what special or unique ways has God shown his love for you?**
* 🌷 **In what ways can you show God's unique love for you to others?**

Invite children to make perfect peanut sandwiches by spreading peanut butter on rice cakes and then using the granola and raisins to decorate the cakes in their own special ways. As you work, discuss how each person is different and special because God made us all as unique individuals. Also talk about the unique ways each child could show God's love to others.

When the cakes are decorated, have children hold them up to show their special designs. Then say: **Before we enjoy our unique treats, let's thank God for his perfect love that helps us love everyone we meet in our own special ways.** Pray: **Dear God, thank you for your perfect love. We love because you first loved us, and you've taught us through your love that we're special. Thank you for the warm, wonderful feeling your love brings to our lives. Amen.**

If there's time, let kids have a peanut judging contest. Rate the peanuts on how big they are, how smooth they appear, how evenly shaped they are, or even how many peanuts are in a shell. Award a blue ribbon to all the perfect peanuts, then hand each child a blue ribbon. Have kids write 1 John 3:1 on the ribbons to remind them that God loves them because they are special in his eyes. Encourage children to use the ribbons as bookmark reminders of how they are uniquely loved by God—and how they can uniquely share God's love with others. 🍎

Power Punch

THE VALUE DU JOUR:
Faith

OOD FOR THOUGHT
With faith, we can change the world! *(Matthew 17:20; Colossians 3:23; James 2:14-18)*

IMPLE INGREDIENTS
You'll need a Bible, resealable plastic bags, a spoon, drinking straws, sparkling apple cider, peppermint extract, cold water, a 1/2-cup measuring cup, and fruit sherbet.

EVOURING THE MESSAGE

Gather kids and hand each a resealable plastic bag. Pour a bit of water into each bag as you say: **You're holding a bag with plain water inside. Not too exciting, is it? Even though water is used for many things, it seems almost impossible to change plain old water into anything exciting. This is often how we view the world and all its problems. Can anything really change the world or the people who live here? Isn't it too big of a job to try and make changes? Think for a moment—what are some of the things in the world you'd like to change but feel helpless to do?** Encourage children to name things such as feelings of hatred, illness, world hunger, severe poverty, and crime.

Then say: **We often think that it's just too hard to change the world—maybe even impossible. So we don't act. We just sit and watch and wait for something or someone else to make a change. But there is someone who can help us change even the most impossible situations! We know that anything is possible through faith in God and his awesome power! And God can help us put our faith into action to change things. All it takes is faith and following God! Let's see what the Bible says about putting our faith into action.**

Read aloud Matthew 17:20b; Colossians 3:23; and James 2:14-18. Then ask:

🍂 **Why is faith without action empty faith?**

🍂 **How can faith in God's power change the world? change lives? bring others to God?**

🍂 **In what ways can we put our faith into action?**

As you continue the lesson, add ingredients to the water in the resealable bags. Say: **Let's see how we can go about changing things through active faith. We can put faith into action through sweetness, kind deeds, and prayer for others.** *(Add a scoop of sherbet.)* **We can put our faith into action by relying on God's sparkling power** *(add 1/2 cup of cider)* **and by the spice of the Holy Spirit.** *(Add a dollop of peppermint extract.)* **Wow! What a recipe for change! Now seal your bag tightly and shake it a bit, then open the corner and slide in a straw to sip. You'll taste how that plain ol' water has been changed!**

As kids sip their drinks, say: **Change doesn't happen by itself, and God usually doesn't just zap changes into place. He wants us to use our hearts and hands to make good changes. God wants us to have active faith that can change the world! Let's offer a prayer asking God's help.** Pray: **Dear God, please help us put our faith into action that will help others and change the world for you! Amen.**

🍎 **TIDBITS** 🍎

What gives sparkle power to sparkling beverages? Plain ol' air! Pressurized air is forced into the liquid. When the millions of bubbles explode, it causes the liquid to sparkle and fizzzzzz!

Encourage kids to make these sparkling, power-packed sipper treats for families and friends to remind them that God's power and our faith in action can change the world.

Jellied Jems

THE VALUE DU JOUR:
Priorities

OOD FOR THOUGHT

God is the most precious part of our lives! *(Psalm 119:72; Romans 11:33; Colossians 2:2)*

IMPLE INGREDIENTS

You'll need a Bible, a spool of thread or new fishing line, new darning needles, and large and small gumdrops.

Before class, be sure you have a darning needle for each child. Cut thread or new fishing line into 20-inch lengths, one for each child. Be sure you have at least twelve gumdrops for each child.

EVOURING THE MESSAGE

Place the needles, thread or fishing line, and gumdrops on a table.
Gather kids and ask them to tell about the most valuable thing they can think of. Is it silver or gold? Jewels or diamonds? Fancy cars or huge mansions?

Allow several minutes for kids to tell their ideas, then say: **There are many valuable things in our world. Some of those are precious stones such as diamonds and rubies. Other valuables might be silver and gold. Some people might consider their time, good health, or their families the most valuable things there are. But there is something far more precious than gold or silver, something far more costly than diamonds or pearls. Do you know who is more**

valuable than any other thing? God! In fact, God is the most precious part of our lives! Listen to what the Bible says about how precious God is. Read aloud Psalm 119:72; Romans 11:33; and Colossians 2:2. Then ask:

- **Why do you think God is the most treasured part of our lives?**
- **How are God's love, power, and grace more precious than silver or gold?**
- **How can we make God our main priority each day? share this great treasure with others?**

Say: **The most valued priority in our lives should be God. In other words, we need to value God above every other person and thing in life. As we discover more about the preciousness of God, let's make precious jewel necklaces to eat and wear.**

Show kids how to use the darning needles to string the gumdrop "gems" onto the thread or fishing line. Have kids slide the gems to the center, stringing twelve gems on the thread. As kids work, have them name one reason why God is treasured, valued, and precious as they slide each gem in place. Then briefly discuss why it's wise to value God and his love above all else in the world.

When the necklaces are complete, have kids tie the ends together and slip the edible gem jewelry over their heads. Then say: **Each time you nibble on a colorful gem, remember that God is the most valuable part of our lives! Now let's share a prayer telling God how much we love and value him.** Pray: **Dear God, you are more precious than silver or gold. You are worth more than any other part of our lives. We love you so much and will always put you first! Amen.**

To help younger children realize the value of God in their lives, have each child make another necklace to present to someone in a younger class. Be sure to explain to the other class that God is more valuable than any gems or gold and that we always want to value God and give him top priority in our lives!

TIDBITS

Kids may enjoy discovering that the promised land of Canaan had many pure deposits of silver and gold, which the Israelites used in making jewelry, weapons, and coins. But the Israelites discovered that no wealth compared to God!

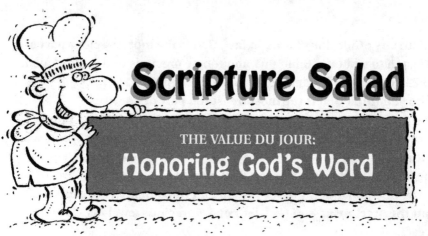

Scripture Salad

THE VALUE DU JOUR:
Honoring God's Word

OOD FOR THOUGHT

We need to learn, speak, and use God's Word in our lives. *(Psalm 119:11; 2 Timothy 3:16; 1 John 2:5)*

IMPLE INGREDIENTS

You'll need a Bible, permanent markers, grated cheese, browned ground beef, lettuce, red plastic bowls, taco sauce, and plastic forks. *Before class, brown and drain a pound of ground beef.*

EVOURING THE MESSAGE

Place the snack ingredients, bowls, and markers on a table. Gather kids and read aloud Psalm 119:11 two times. Then ask kids to repeat the verse with you. Finally, ask for volunteers to recite the Scripture and tell what they think God is saying to us in this verse.

Then say: **We hear and say thousands of words every day, but the most important words we'll ever hear, speak, or use are God's words to us in his Word. Some people think that it's only important to know the gist of what God says or that it's not really useful to learn God's Word by heart. But that's not true. God wants us to do three things with his Word. God wants us to learn, speak, and use his Word every day of our lives. Listen to what God says in his Word.** Read aloud 2 Timothy 3:16 and 1 John 2:5, then ask:

🍎 In what ways is God's Word useful to us every day?

🍎 Why is it important to do *all* three things: to learn, speak, and use God's Word? Why isn't doing one of these enough?

🍎 How can you work to learn, speak, and use God's Word?

Hand each child a red bowl to represent a heart. Have kids use markers to write "Psalm 119:11" on the bowls. As kids fill their bowls with salad, continue the lesson: **We can almost think of God's Word as a Scripture Salad to put in our hearts and use in our lives. Green lettuce represents learning God's Word and how it helps us grow and live. Cheese is nutritious for us, just as Scripture feeds us God's truth. It represents understanding and digesting God's Word. The meat is what gives us energy to use in our lives, just as Scripture provides energy to our spirits and empowers us to put God's Word into use. Taco sauce is spicy and represents the excitement we feel in learning God's truth! Before we dig into these nutritious and delicious salad snacks, let's thank God for his nutritious Word!**

Pray: **Dear God, thank you for your Word, which gives us truth and life as you intended. Please help us want to learn, speak, and use your Word every day. Amen.**

As kids nibble their Scripture Salads, have them discuss why just memorizing or simply knowing the gist of God's Word isn't enough. Guide kids to discover that we need to learn, speak, and use Scripture to show the importance and value of God's Word! When kids finish eating, wash out the bowls and let kids take them home as reminders that God's Word is not only nutritious for our lives but also delicious!

Color With Joy!

THE VALUE DU JOUR:

Appreciation

OOD FOR THOUGHT

Let's appreciate the small things God does. *(Psalm 136:1-9; 1 Thessalonians 5:18)*

IMPLE INGREDIENTS

You'll need a Bible, scissors, white poster board, licorice sticks, gel icing in various colors, and graham crackers or large soda-cracker squares.

Before class, enlarge and photocopy the palette illustration below to use as a pattern. Trace the pattern on poster board and cut out a palette for each child. If kids are older, let them trace and cut the patterns. Be sure to cut out thumb holes as indicated on the pattern!

DEVOURING THE MESSAGE

Set out the snack ingredients, then gather kids and say: **Let's begin by playing a fun game. We'll slap our knees two times, then clap our hands twice, then snap our fingers two times. When we're familiar with the rhythm, we'll go around the circle and each person can name a color after the snap-snap. For example, we'll go "slap-slap, clap-clap, snap-snap, red!" Let's see how many colors we can name! As a hint, think of the colors of nature or of the colors in your crayon boxes!**

Play until you've named all the colors you can think of. Then hook your thumb in a poster-board palette and say: **Think of all the colors God used to paint the world so beautifully! There's the dewy green of new spring grass, the sparkling blue of the sky and its reflection on water—and just think of the soft orange blush of fresh, ripe peaches! Colors are something we often take for granted since we see them all the time. But just imagine how boring every-thing would be if God hadn't created colors! How do you think we should respond to all of God's creative coloring? Let's see what God's Word says.** Read aloud Psalm 136:1-9 and 1 Thessalonians 5:18. Then ask:

🍎 **Why is it important to recognize even the small things God does?**
🍎 **What would life be like without the touches of beauty God gives us?**
🍎 **How can we take time to appreciate all the things God does for us?**

Say: **Living a lifestyle of appreciation and thankfulness for all God gives to us is important. When we have a sense of appreciation, we feel happy, peaceful, and content with what we have. Let's paint pictures with special tools to thank God for his wonderful gifts and to show our appreciation for all he does.**

Hand each child a poster-board palette and a licorice stick. Show kids how to nibble one end of the sticks and bite them gently to fray the ends into "paintbrushes." Then squeeze a small dollop of each color of gel icing onto the palettes and have kids paint a thank-you card to God on a large cracker. As kids work, challenge them to name things God made that we sometimes take for granted, things such as air, the sun rising, tiny but interesting insects, and even rain!

When the edible thank-you's are done, invite kids to explain their designs. Then close with a prayer asking God to help you nurture a lifestyle of appreciation for the world and all God has made for us! 🍎

No-Fear Bananas

THE VALUE DU JOUR:
Confidence

OOD FOR THOUGHT
We're not fearful because God is with us. *(Joshua 1:9; Psalm 118:6)*

IMPLE INGREDIENTS
You'll need a Bible, paper plates, tubes of frosting in a variety of colors, and a banana for each child.

EVOURING THE MESSAGE
Set out the tubes of frosting and paper plates. Gather kids and hand each a banana. Ask kids to use their bananas as microphones as they tell about times they felt afraid or alone.

Then say: **We all have times when it's hard to be brave or not feel lonely. But I have a wonderful secret that I'm going to share with you so you'll never need to be afraid again! The secret is in a special Bible story I'll tell you. And you can help tell the story with your bananas! Just listen as I tell the story and follow along with your bananas.**

Once there was a young boy named David. David loved to play his harp *(strum the bananas)* and write poems or psalms. *(Pretend to write with the bananas.)* But most of all, David loved God and knew God was number one in his life! *(Hold the bananas high.)* However, a mean giant named Goliath didn't love God. See him scowl? *(Hold the bananas like frowns.)* Grrrr!

David wanted to stop Goliath from making fun of God, but he was so much smaller than the giant! *(Stand the bananas on the floor.)* But God saw David in a different way. God looked inside David and saw a giant heart of love! *(Peel the bananas half way down.)* David wasn't afraid of the mean giant—do you know why? Because David loved God and knew that God was with him! Yeah! *(Gently shake the bananas in the air.)* So David used his sling to kill Goliath— and the mean giant couldn't scare anyone again! *(Wave the bananas back and forth a few times.)*

Have kids sit and hold their bananas. Read aloud Joshua 1:9 and Psalm 118:6a, then ask:

🍌 Why does God not want us to be afraid?

🍌 How can knowing God is with us make us brave? keep us from feeling alone?

🍌 What monsters make you afraid? How can you give those fears to God?

Say: **Remember I had a secret way never to be afraid? Well, God is that secret! When we love and trust God and know he's with us, we don't have to be afraid—God can handle any fear! Let's make Goliath Bananas, then gobble them up to show we're not afraid of anything with God on our side!**

Invite kids to decorate their half-peeled bananas with frosting, then show everyone the silly Goliaths they made! Before gobbling Goliath, close with a prayer thanking God for his continual presence and the fact that we don't have to live with a spirit of fear.

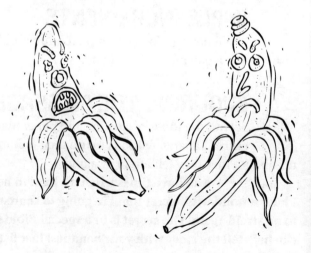

If you have time (and enough bananas) consider presenting this object talk to a younger class to remind them that we have no fear with God on our side. Then help the younger children make funny Goliaths. They'll go bananas! 🍎

Tasty Trees

OOD FOR THOUGHT

We want our lives to be rooted in God! *(Psalm 1:1-3; Matthew 13:1-9)*

IMPLE INGREDIENTS

You'll need a Bible, carrot sticks, 1/2 pound broccoli florets, 1/2 pound fresh asparagus spears, 1/8 cup orange juice, sesame seeds, 1/4 cup olive oil, and salt.

Before class, clean and cut carrot sticks into long "tree trunks." Wash the broccoli florets and asparagus, but don't cut the asparagus. Prepare Fun Fertilizer Dip by whipping the orange juice, olive oil, and sesame seeds, then salt to taste. If you have time, your kids will enjoy the preparation as much as the munching!

EVOURING THE MESSAGE

Set the snack ingredients on a table. Hold up a carrot and place a broccoli floret on top. Ask kids what they think you've made. Then say: **Don't these vegetables remind you of a tree? Trees of all shapes and sizes are all around us. And although leaves or the sizes of trees and bushes may be different, there's one thing they all have in common. Do you know what it is?**

Allow kids to tell their ideas, then say: **All trees have something big and powerful to keep them anchored in the ground and to prevent them from falling over. All trees have deep roots! Did you know that God wants us to be like trees with deep roots? Tree roots are firmly planted in the ground, but our roots are to be firmly planted in God! What do you think that means?**

Let children share their ideas, then read aloud the parable of the seeds from Matthew 13:1-9. Ask:

🍎 **How are we like plants with roots?**

🍎 **Why do you think deep roots are important for trees? for us?**

♥ What might happen if our roots of faith aren't strong or deep?

♥ How can we strengthen and deepen our roots of commitment to God?

Say: **Think of a tree out in a field. If its roots aren't strong and deep and a huge storm wind comes huffing and puffing, what will happen to the tree? It falls down! Our lives are the same way. If our faith in and commitment to God aren't strong and deep, when troubles come along—and they always do—then we may not be strong enough to stand against them. Our faith may weaken, and we might fall—and that would be awful! Let's make some strong, tasty trees to munch on. They'll also remind us that our own lives must be rooted in God!**

Show kids how to make bushy elm trees with broccoli and carrots or strong, tall palm trees using asparagus spears. Dip the treetops and trunks in the Fun Fertilizer Dip and explain that, just as trees need to be fed to be strong and have deep roots, our faith needs to be fed with God's Word and truth!

When the last trees are crunched, gather everyone in a circle and lock elbows. Lean backward and let the strength of the other "roots" keep everyone from falling. Slowly return to an upright position and say: **Let's share a prayer asking God to help us grow strong roots of commitment to him so we can stand strong for him in any situation.** Pray: **Dear Lord, we thank you for your love and strength. Please help us grow our roots of faith in you so we will be able to stand against anything! Amen.** End by reading aloud Psalm 1:1-3. ♥